AWARENESS.
CLARITY.
POWER.

JILL S. MacDONALD

GoWith-IN
THE SERIES

ISBN: 978-1-7337955-8-6

Edited by: Libby Wiersema and Amy Ashby

Warren
publishing

Published by Warren Publishing
Charlotte, NC
www.warrenpublishing.net
Printed in the United States

*This book, and all the books in this series,
are dedicated to my Dream Team.*

*You know who you are. You've believed in me
since day one. I am the luckiest person to be loved
by you all. I need nothing else to be the truth of who
I am and share that with the world. Thank you for
reminding me to shine my light. Your light shines
on me every day and I am SO grateful.*

*To my readers: I've thought about you for years while
I was writing. I am so excited you're holding
my first book! It is my greatest hope that this book
will lighten your load, bring you ease, and remind
you of who you are … a light in this world.*

Contents.

Welcome.

This book has found its way into your hands at just the right time.

It is my pleasure to take you on this journey of gentle awakening, ah-ha moments, and a closer connection and alignment to yourself.

Read whatever draws you in. Filter it with your own wisdom and guidance. My joy lies in your ah-ha moments, the feeling of relief when you read something that resonates as truth, and the clarity that comes when you are more aware of who you are and what you want.

No one's voice matters more for you than yours. No one can create power within you but you. And no one can take your power away unless you give them permission. I hope this little book inspires you to take your power back in whatever ways you've (unintentionally) given it away.

Sit back. Relax. Slowly take in this little book of insights and its gentle gems of wisdom. It has been written with the energy and intention to speak directly to each reader. It will meet you where you are right now, and assist you in awakening more of who you are. This book is a personal journey you're ready to take because it found its way into your hands.

All the answers you need come from within. I hope this book will help you to remember and trust this truth. I will be here every step of the way. This book is my gift to you.

A suggestion for reading: Read a section and allow it to settle into you. Journal if you are inspired by the topic, and meditate on anything that surfaces strongly for you.

Be gentle with yourself. Awakening is not always easy. Know your higher self will guide you to become aware of whatever you're ready to become aware of in the now moment—nothing more, nothing less.

No one's voice matters
more for you than yours.
No one can create
power within you
but you. And no one
can take your power
away unless you give
them permission.

Introduction.

We all need self-awareness to have clarity. And self-awareness requires some time, attention, and focus. There is no better investment or bigger return, because the clarity we receive from awareness is the foundation of our personal power. We require that power in order to create the life we truly desire.

Growing up, we are taught many things that give our power away. We are taught to be pleasers, not to question authority, not to question the beliefs we are taught within our families, societies, or religions.

We are not encouraged to think independently in our schools, and sometimes not in our homes either. We are taught we need to be concerned with what other people think. All these things create a separation from ourselves and in turn, give our power away. When we wake up to our greater awareness and clarity, our power begins to return. We begin to think, to speak, and to behave in alignment with our truth. We make choices from the center of our being. That is power.

Awareness + Clarity = Power.

This life is ours to live any way we choose; to enjoy pure happiness, connection, abundance, wellness, well-being, joy, inspiration, expansion, and love. It is my hope and intention to assist you in becoming more of who you are and who you want to be, in order to live the life of your dreams. Your dreams are your dreams for a reason. They are your soul calling out to you. Absolutely nothing is impossible. The word impossible also says, "I'm possible." We just need to learn how to get out of our own way.

So let's talk about what is possible....

When we wake up
to our greater
awareness and clarity,
our power begins
to return.

What Does It Mean to Be Aware?

We were born with awareness. But we are raised away from that awareness.

Awareness is a connection to your higher self, your truth, and the purpose you came here to live. The question then becomes, how do we lose sight of that knowing? The answer lies in how we were raised. Through no fault of their own, our parents gave us their beliefs, their thoughts, and their intentions for us. The operative word being "their." However, their thoughts, beliefs, and intentions are not necessarily ours. The blank canvas of your life is yours to paint. Yet, it is not well-known (or common) to raise a child to be trusted with their own journey. Parents believe they know better. But do they really? Can anybody ever really know what is best for another human being?

Kids are often told by their parents that they can live their own lives when they move out of the house. The problem comes when (for eighteen-plus years) they have been told what to think, feel, how to behave, what to do ... because parenting is often confused with indoctrination. Though mostly unintentional, this is a reality of the most common parenting paradigm.

We cannot discover who we are by being told who we should be. Ask parents what they want most for their child(ren) and they will say, "happiness." Yet to be happy, we must know who we are, be aware, and be free to challenge the thoughts and beliefs we were given. Once we have that awareness, we can choose what is best for us. That choice cannot occur if we never question the beliefs we were given.

To be awake requires awareness. Awareness requires clarity. And clarity comes from listening to the voice within us. To hear that voice requires the stillness, space, and freedom to explore who we are apart from society, friends, family, and those who raise(d) us. Learning to listen from within is where the journey of awakening begins, expands, and thrives.

To be awake requires
awareness. Awareness
requires clarity.
And clarity comes
from listening to the
voice within us.

What Is Clarity?

Clarity is deep, unwavering knowing. Clarity is a portal to your personal power. Without clarity, we unintentionally give our power away to everything and everyone outside of us.

Clarity is the foundation from which we launch—otherwise we are just ships in the ocean, blowing with the wind, unable to control the sails. Clarity is freedom from doubt and fear. Clarity is consciousness.

Meditate for a few days on the word "clarity" and feel the energy in it. Explore what clarity feels like to you. No one can give you clarity or explain it for you, because clarity is an individual experience. But you know it when you feel it. To sense your clarity (on whatever the topic) may require becoming quiet and placing more focus on your inner being.

Most of us have had the experience (at least once in our lives) of being so certain about something that nothing could sway us. That is clarity. The more, the better. Your ability to create the life you most want to live lies in your focus and willingness to create as much clarity as possible. Clarity allows you to build a life that lines up to the truth of who you are and why you are here.

Clarity is worth your time and attention. Focus on that intention, ask your higher self for more clarity, and see what comes. Enjoy the exploration. Know you will come up against resistance to the beliefs you were given if you find they do not fit. That's ok. Be easy about it. Clarity grows stronger and builds a solid foundation when we hold it up against anything we've been told or taught that is not in alignment.

This is an internal process of evolving … evolving more and more into who we are beyond what we are told, taught, and see outside of ourselves.

Most of us have had
the experience (at least
once in our lives) of
being so certain
about something that
nothing could sway us.
That is clarity.

What Is Power?

Personal power comes as a natural result of greater awareness and inner clarity.

Most humans live their lives without much awareness. Most live more on the surface of things. Yet awareness cannot be discovered on the surface. Nor are we here, capable of everything we are capable of, to lack awareness. But awareness is not automatic—it is an experience that requires an ongoing commitment to self-observation, nonjudgement, and the desire for self-discovery. What could possibly be more interesting to you than yourself? You are an amazing creature here on Earth, at this time, for a reason and a purpose.

So, let's get back to the idea of power, which emerges through both awareness and clarity. Once we choose to wake up, we uncover more inner clarity and can then begin to act on it; this is when the magic starts happening. There is incredible, unstoppable power within each of us. It is a well that has no bottom. It only appears to run dry because we give away what we have.

What does it mean to give away our power? It means we look to others, to situations, to relationships, to outcomes, to circumstances in order to validate, acknowledge, measure, gauge ... what resides within us. The circumstances, situations, relationships, and outcomes in our lives are reflections from within. The simplest way to know you've given away your power is by how you feel. It never feels good to give away our power, and it always feels good to tap into it. Most of us have experienced moments when we knew we stood in our power, felt our alignment, and listened to our guidance. Utilize those moments to assist you in accessing your power more often. Notice when you give your power away (allowing someone to upset you, personalizing situations, telling stories) and notice when you stand grounded in your power (making choices that feel right, knowing which action is right to take, being in the moment, seeing results that resonate).

You are powerful beyond measure.
Remember that.

There is incredible,
unstoppable power
within each of us.
It is a well that has
no bottom.

Everything Happens with a Reason.

Nature is incredible. Seasons come and go effortlessly, trees shed leaves when they need to, and buds re-emerge in spring. Rain comes to water all the plant life and the growth never ends. Our bodies are incredible in the same way nature is. Our eyes blink without effort, our skin heals from abrasions on its own, and, from birth, we grow and evolve continuously.

There is a design to nature and our bodies. There is also a design to our individual evolution. We have been gifted with tools like intuition, sensory abilities, feelings, and inner guidance for a purpose. We are here purposefully just as nature is—designed to evolve, thrive, and connect to all that is. Have you ever noticed how much better you feel when you are outdoors in nature? We are a part of that design, and it connects us to the Earth and to ourselves.

Everything happens with a reason. Our job is not to dig for the reason, but to instead allow the wisdom of that knowing to permeate our daily lives, our thoughts, our intentions, and our actions. You must develop a deep, quiet trust in life. A trust of nature. A trust of your body. A trust in your purpose for being here. That wisdom changes everything.

This world was not randomly designed; there is a flow to it. We were not randomly designed, either. There is a flow to us. The more we open to accessing our own flow, the more we see the powerful synchronization of our lives. Looking deeper into nature and our incredible bodies allows us to sense that rhythm and tap into it.

We can connect more deeply through our breath. Breathing deeply and focusing your mind on your breath (and only your breath) brings you into the now moment. If it doesn't the first time, repeat until it does. Be patient with yourself. If your thoughts tend to race, and most people's do, just continue to bring your focus back to your breath.

Our job is not to discover the reason for everything, but rather to live it. Therein lies the magic. To trust. To believe. To connect. To listen. To allow. To receive.

Everything happens with a reason. Nature does not resist—it flows. We are here to flow with life, not to resist it.

Everything happens
with a reason.
Our job is not to
dig for the reason,
but to instead allow
the wisdom of that
knowing to permeate
our daily lives…

To Flow with Life.

What does it mean to flow with life?

We make choices in every moment and don't even realize it. Every thought is either a thought of allowing or a thought of resisting. These thoughts then influence the actions we take and the decisions we make. Each choice is made with an energy of allowing or an energy of resisting—and the results reflect that state of being.

To become aware of whether you are allowing or resisting, you need to observe yourself. When you take time to slow down, tap in, get quiet, you begin to sense, feel, and know your inner being. That knowing (clarity) allows you to see deeper into your thoughts and beliefs. Thoughts can run away from you easily and take you on a ride that leads you far away from yourself. Remember, you are not the thoughts you think, but rather, the awareness behind those thoughts.

Most people's thoughts tend to be resistant in nature—more negative (fearful) than positive (trusting). We are taught to believe the answers we seek come from the mind, but they do not.

Figuring out a math problem comes from the mind, but figuring out ourselves does not.

To flow with life, rather than against it, we have to tune into our own rhythm. Within that rhythm lies our flow. To flow with your rhythm, you need to know yourself. To know yourself, you need to get out of the mind. The truth of yourself will always emerge in the stillness. Throughout the day, catch your thoughts. Observe them. Ask yourself if that thought is yours or someone else's (society, friends, family, etc.).

Any thought that doesn't feel good is not flowing with life. Trees don't get upset when their leaves fall. They just allow it. We resist because we think rather than flow. Notice when you measure, evaluate, judge ... this is resistance. Look around at what is, and see if you can allow it to be, without judgment.

To flow with life is a way of life. There is no destination to reach. We all know people who are wadded up with stress, expectations, and judgment. Maybe this is you, but that's ok. Begin to recognize your resistance, and it will begin to ease. A bit of awareness goes a long way. Focus on flowing with life rather than against it, and see what that experience feels like.

To flow with life, rather than against it, we have to tune into our own rhythm. Within that rhythm lies our flow. To flow with your rhythm, you need to know yourself.

Intentional and Unintentional Creations.

We are creators. In every moment, we create—whether we know it or not. Once we become more aware, we begin to see the connections between intentional and unintentional creations. For example, have you ever noticed on a not-so-good day, more and more not-so-good things pop up into your experience? Or when you are so in love, how everything seems to flow, falling easily into place, and all is right with the world? This is not accidental. This is part of our design. We are all energetic beings who create with our thoughts, words, intentions, and actions.

Here is a great example you will feel immediately. In our community there are signs that say:

Hate Has No Home Here.

Take a moment to sense those words.

Now feel these words:

Love Lives Here.

Notice a difference? Huge difference. Pretty cool, huh? This discernment is where our power resides. How is that where our power lies, you ask? Because this is a universe that responds to energy, focus, and intention. We create based on what we focus on. The Universe does not hear the word "no." It responds to what we focus on. So, if you say "I hate hatred," you are focused on hate. This is precisely how we unintentionally create things we do not want in our lives, only to feel baffled about how we arrived there. This one awareness is life-altering and taps you into your deepest potential and immense personal power.

What are you focusing on?

We are all energetic
beings who create with
our thoughts, words,
intentions, and actions.

Whatever We Focus on Grows.

To know the full range of our power, we need to be aware that whatever we focus on grows. Like sunlight to a flower, our attention on a subject makes it grow and expand. Have you ever noticed when you're really angry at someone, they just make you more angry? Or when you focus on what you don't like about someone, that's all you see? The opposite is also equally true: when you see the best in someone, that is your predominant experience with them.

Whatever we focus on grows. But don't take my word for it, experiment for yourself. Nothing matters more than our own experience. And experience is our only teacher. Just observe yourself for a few days. When you feel crappy, ask yourself: what am I focusing on? Where are my thoughts? And when you feel great, do the same. Patterns will emerge and you will become more familiar with what you're really focusing on. Then you can begin to consciously choose what you want to focus on. Most of us are completely unaware of where our focus is because we are not taught to pay attention.

Once you begin to pay closer attention, your awareness will increase and you will feel the power of influence. You will also begin to see that whatever you focus on grows.

Most of us are
completely unaware
of where our focus is
because we are not
taught to pay attention.

Allow Life to Wake You.

We go through life asleep or awake—awake to ourselves and the bigger picture (events, circumstances, experiences)—or not. Being awake to a bigger picture is not automatic. In fact, human functioning is more closely associated with being asleep than awake. Through no fault of our own, we do not question this experience until something jolts us awake.

Through our life experiences, and the emotions we feel toward those experiences, we gradually wake up when we choose to. We begin to desire clarity and seek it. Once you choose to awaken, you have already begun the process. When we consciously claim responsibility for ourselves, our perceptions, our reactions, our stories, this choice changes our paradigm. Most humans act as if we're all living the same reality. But in actuality, we are each experiencing our own reality.

Ask new questions. Foster curiosity. Engage with people who have a broader perspective. Challenge your beliefs. Life will support you. It can be a gentle experience. Be gentle with yourself. Allow life to awaken you to *you*.

Empower Yourself.

We each have our own energetic signature. Our imprint on the world within us and around us is an ongoing, never-ending, unfolding, expansive template. We expand collectively as a human consciousness, and as individuals.

Nothing is permanent. Everything is always changing. Life is change. In order to be in the flow with life, we need to find the channels within us that are empowering to us. This is a unique experience. What rings your bell and what rings mine may differ greatly. We "vibe with our tribe," as they say, and as important as it is to find your tribe, it is important to know your vibe. Tapping into that energy is empowering. When you come to observe what you feel passionate about, what rings your bell, what connects you to a greater purpose, and what connects you to yourself and the world, you begin to know your vibe. This vibe is uniquely you, designed to assist you to live in alignment with yourself.

This uniquely human experience is one that requires awareness. It requires curiosity and interest in oneself. Once we turn on this curiosity, sense our unique signature, and understand our intentions for being here at this time and place, we become more alive. We begin to notice judgments of ourselves and others—and how limiting and pointless they are—we begin to drop stories and see they are just that: stories. We grow into a deeper relationship with ourselves and adopt a kinder, gentler perspective on ourselves and others.

Find some quiet time to go within, get quiet and listen. Notice how full your inner world is, just waiting for you to look within. Honor your own energetic signature; it is your contribution to the world. You being you is the most important contribution you can make. Watch your authenticity increase, your masks fall away, and a freedom arise within you. Be the powerhouse you came here to be.

Life is change.
In order to be in the
flow with life, we need
to find the channels
within us that are
empowering to us.

Abundance or Lack?

Nature is abundant. Growth is a never-ending cycle of rebirth. We are abundant creatures full of unlimited potential, wellness, and well-being. Abundance is our natural orientation. Lack is learned.

Look to any young child and you can see how abundance is their orientation—they know anything is possible, until that knowing is taught out of them. Many of us were taught a 'not enough' mentality. We are all told to face reality rather than create it. We are taught limitation, not unlimited power. These teachings are the beginning of a limited, lack-oriented frame of mind. This lack orientation is deeply ingrained into most human beings.

Our lack orientation is responsible for influencing our perspectives, our relationships, our experiences, our health, and ultimately, our happiness and fulfillment (or lack thereof) in life. This one orientation—abundance or lack—powerfully shapes every experience of our lives. Thus it is well worth a closer look.

Spend a few days observing yourself and the world around you. Observe conversations, interactions, thoughts, and experiences that come from a perspective of abundance or lack. Be gentle with these observations (especially your thoughts), because sometimes it is a bit daunting to wake up to how strongly held this lack perspective may be. But fear not—anything can be changed through awareness, clarity, and effort.

Enjoy the observation process. It is fascinating. It can lead to new, conscious choices—and a more abundant orientation toward yourself, your experiences, your health, your well-being, your relationships, and your life.

We are abundant
creatures full
of unlimited
potential, wellness,
and well-being.

Everything Is Here to Assist You.

Everything is here to help you.

Yes, everything.

We are not always capable of seeing the bigger picture. Sometimes in hindsight, we become aware, but hindsight arrives layer by layer and can take years to unfold completely. Faith is necessary if we are to believe anything bigger is unfolding. Regardless of your particular beliefs (which are very personal in nature), the important thing is that something taps you into that bigger picture.

Faith is believing in the unseen, the unprovable, and the unquantifiable. Some of our most powerful beliefs are unseen, unprovable, and unquantifiable. Yet most humans want proof before they'll believe in anything. If something isn't provable, it is difficult for most to believe. Needing proof is a mind-based perspective. Faith lives beyond the mind. Faith is the belief in the unprovable. We are so much more than our mind-generated thoughts. To live only in the mind cuts off our accessibility to our higher senses and awareness.

For in your heart lies wisdom and a higher connection to yourself and others. From your heart-center you can access unlimited faith. Often when tragic things occur, we organically drop into our hearts and our higher knowing to get through it. Yet, we can access our heart-centered consciousness anytime by taking deep breaths and dropping our awareness into our hearts. Then we can proceed on.

Give it a try. Close your eyes and take three slow, deep breaths. Feel yourself drop your awareness into your heart. Feel a shift? If you don't, repeat until you do feel a calm shift. Then open your eyes and proceed onto your next task. See how that feels for you.

We all have the innate ability to get quiet and tap into higher intelligence, higher awareness, and more intuitive knowing and guidance. Once we tune into this higher awareness, we begin to know that everything has a benefit. Everything has a reason. Everything is here to help us. Everything is a piece of a bigger picture.

Breathe into your own deeper knowing and see where it takes you.

Use your breath to assist you. You will find much peace there.

Understanding, knowing, sensing, feeling, and accepting that everything is here to assist you will relax your body, decrease your stress, improve your health, and allow room for more joy.

Be Easy About It.

We humans seem to feel hassled over just about everything. We argue, fight, resist, rage, rebel, and protest. We fight traffic, we get annoyed about standing in line, and we grow more and more impatient with ourselves and each other.

Nature does not resist.

Animals do not resist.

Only humans, "the thinking creatures," resist.

We are filled with resistance. Our bodies are tensed up. Tension is resistance.

Why do we think it's a good idea to argue, to fight against, to resist and rage, to rebel and protest our way through our lives?

Sometimes we behave like adults having tantrums.

What if that is not such a beneficial choice? What if we are (unintentionally) making life much harder on ourselves?

Yes. We are.

Be easier with yourself.

Introduce gentleness into your daily life.

Slow your roll.

Try adopting ease as a new approach to your day.

Take more intentional and deeper breaths.

Before reacting to anything, create some space. Breathe first and say gently to yourself, "be easy about this." You may be pleasantly surprised by the ease you feel and the more mindful choices that follow.

Take more
intentional and
deeper breaths.

Gratitude: Our Superpower.

Has anyone ever asked you, "if you could have one superpower, what would it be?" People inevitably think of things like the abilities to fly, read other people's minds, become invisible, etc. Little do we know, we all have easy access to a superpower.

That superpower is gratitude.

Humans have the unique ability to deeply appreciate. We have the power to align our thoughts and emotions to create profound effects on our experiences. Doesn't sound like a superpower to you? Well, it is! Allow me to expand on how this ability is profound enough that I call it a superpower.

We are energetic beings, first and foremost. Our energy is capable of being harnessed and utilized in any way we choose. Most humans do not realize that first, we are energetic beings, and second, we can learn to use this energy for our greater good. This ability to harness our energy is not widely known or taught in our homes, schools, or places of employment.

We are each capable of harnessing our energy in any way we choose. The best way to experiment and experience the impact of your energy and ability to harness it is to practice gratitude. What does that mean? It means consciously choosing to deeply appreciate something (or someone) each and every day.

When we intentionally focus on a strong feeling of appreciation (rather than just the thought of appreciation), we shift our energy. For example, if it is a tough day and it's hard to find something to appreciate, look around you. Something as simple as taking a drink of water can become a focus of gratitude. The key is not what you appreciate, but that you appreciate, consciously acknowledging and feeling appreciation all at once. Another example: when someone you love hugs you, fully feel the embrace. At the same time, appreciate the person and that moment. Last example (and a very easy one): when you first lie in bed at night after a long day, notice and feel the mattress beneath you, smell the scent of the sheets, and appreciate the rest and quiet that surrounds you. When practiced consistently, gratitude becomes your superpower because it alters your perspective—which in turn alters your experiences.

We have the power
to align our thoughts
and emotions
to create profound
effects on
our experiences.

Conclusions Are Illusions.

The human mind wants to draw conclusions. The mind will pull us into the illusion that there is a conclusion to find, to discover, to figure out. This illusion/conclusion cycle can grip us for a lifetime.

We have all heard life described as a journey, not a destination. This points us to the idea that there is no conclusion to find—just an unfolding journey to experience. But, what is the journey? The journey is being alive and in the experience of each new moment. We are living, breathing, ever-expanding beings. Nothing exists but this moment. Therefore, is our time well spent expending mental energy trying to force conclusions? What if we meet each moment anew, trusting ourselves rather than drawing conclusions?

We are not our thoughts. We are the awareness behind the thoughts. So, in order to come into alignment with our true selves, we must go beyond the mind, beyond our thoughts, and definitely beyond drawing conclusions.

Mind-based conclusions are made of thoughts, external beliefs, rules, pros and cons, expectations, judgments, society, etc. Your mind wants to come to clear conclusions in order to navigate life. Yet, we are ever-changing, ever-expanding beings. Is it then in our highest good to navigate our lives based on conclusions we determine in our minds that continually change, shift, and evolve? Or might it be a better choice to become more comfortable in the unknown? Might it be a better idea to allow the fluidity of ideas, feelings, and experiences to unfold without drawing conclusions? Humans look for security in drawing conclusions. It's as if conclusions will wrap things up into neat and predictable patterns. This is an illusion, not security. Our security (so to speak) lies in knowing who we are at the deepest level and remembering who we are beyond who we were told to be. Release the need to draw conclusions. Instead, be present in the experience of each new moment. Develop a deeper trust with your inner being, your inspired actions, and your alignment to your higher self.

The journey is being
alive and in the
experience of
each new moment.
We are living, breathing,
ever-expanding beings.

To Feel Alive, Eat Food That Is Alive.

Food is intended to be an energy source for the body. Yet not all that we consume creates energy. The difference between food that creates energy and food that zaps it is whether or not the food being consumed is alive.

To feel energetic, we must consume food that is alive. Food that is alive has energy. It holds a life force in it. When we consume food that has life force energy in it, we feel energized. Uncooked, raw fruits, vegetables, nuts, herbs, and seeds—any foods the sun grows—are alive. These sun- and earth-made edibles contain life-force energy just as we do.

Experiment for yourself. Add into your daily diet more raw foods and see how you feel. Be simple about it—add in an apple, a healthy trail mix, or a fresh salad. Pay attention to how you feel after you eat anything, how you feel when you mix different food groups together in one sitting, and how you feel when you consume raw vs. cooked foods. Once we cook our foods, they are no longer alive. We still receive nutrients from cooked food, just fewer.

There is no one right way—there is only your way. Each person, each body, is unique. The key is to pay closer attention. Your body will tell you what feels best for you if you place your focus there. Our bodies are incredible machines designed to support us. The key is learning how to best support your machine.

When we consume
food that has
life force energy in it,
we feel energized.

The "Sign" in Significant.

Have you ever noticed the base of the word significant is sign? There is a sign/significance for each of us in each moment of our lives. The trick is knowing what is significant and what is not for you—an answer that cannot be found outside of you. True significance can only be discovered within.

Humans struggle with knowing what is significant (worth our time and attention) and what is insignificant (not worth our time and attention). Our society pretends to make much significant that is not. Additionally, we are told what is significant by others right from childhood—rather than being guided to the answers that come from within us.

So much is portrayed by our society as being significant that actually is not. For example, what other people think of you is portrayed as significant, yet it is not. How much money you make, the home you live in, the car you drive, your social status, how many likes you get, how many followers you have are all portrayed as significant, but they are not. Just those few examples are insignificant details of a life that is far more significant than that. As a society, we are drowning in insignificance. The solution is to ground yourself in your connection with yourself. There is nothing stronger than that foundation.

There is a powerful shift that occurs when we see from a broader perspective what is (and what is not) significant and worth our time and attention. Anything that is ego-, mind-, or status-based is insignificant to your being, your essence, your purpose, your higher self—your soul. Spending your life focused on the insignificant can cause great unhappiness and suffering.

Each of us has an ego (mind) and serves a purpose. Yet the mind pretends to make things significant that are not. The ego is not intended to be the driver of our lives or our choices—nor the decider of what is significant. The driver of your life is intended to be your highest self. How do we know this? Because choices made from your highest self bring deep peace and fulfillment. Once you choose to tap into your higher awareness (which is accessible within the silence/stillness) your choices and perspective will broaden, come into alignment with your being, and you will have the ability to clearly see and feel what's important to you, to your relationships, and to your time.

Have you ever noticed how when a tragedy happens, everyone immediately realizes what is most significant, and everything else falls away?

Yet do we need tragedy to function from a place of significance? We can choose differently right now. We simply need the awareness, clarity, focus, and intention to do so. This one choice—to function from a place of significance—can lead to a life of deep fulfillment. Each and every one of us is capable of this daily, moment-by-moment shift.

Life Is Not about What You Measure.

Once we have lived this thing called life long enough, most humans come to the realization that life is about more than meets the eye.

Perhaps life is more than the grades you get in school, the car you drive, the town you're from, the group you hang out with, the home you live in, who you marry, the status of your job, your looks, your social media likes, or your bank account.

But how does all this measuring even begin? And can we be caught up in it without knowing we are? It is worth pondering. How do we as humans come to measure our actual worth based on external factors? How is that belief developed and how is it perpetuated? It is a fascinating exploration into the mind, our society, the media, social media, and the powerful (often unconscious) belief systems that are passed on from one generation to another. Without this basic awareness, it is impossible to go deeper.

If you have ever found yourself caught up in comparison, you know it doesn't feel good.

Life is not about anything we measure. We are not measurable commodities. We are not here to prove our worth. We are not here to prove anything. We are here to be the highest expression of ourselves—and that has no measure.

You were born with limitless worth. That worth is intrinsic, a given, un-earn-able. You have nothing to prove. You are here to be the most authentic expression of yourself; no more no less. You are a human *being*. Not a human *doing*. The sooner you allow yourself to stop measuring, the freer you will be. You will be in your own lane. You will be free to be you.

Children who are raised not to place themselves on a measuring stick—especially by their parents—have permission to become more authentic human beings. Authenticity creates happiness and wellbeing. We are not born measuring, we are taught into it. Once we see and know that, we can reprogram our beliefs and our perspectives. The only requirement for this internal shift is to recognize when you're measuring, acknowledge it for what it is, release it, and move on with your day.

When we stop measuring, we have the freedom and space to be the fullest expression of ourselves. Your life is not about what can be measured. It is so much more.

You were born with
limitless worth.
That worth is intrinsic,
a given, un-earn-able.
You have nothing
to prove.

A Balance of Doing and Being.

We live in a society that has far more reverence for doing than being. We place more value on productivity than relaxation, and prioritize stress over presence. And now, even our kids are being raised in an over-scheduled world as if they will miss out on something if they are not occupied every single second of the day. But what if what our kids are missing out on is knowing who they are separate from what they do? And what if, in a society of constant doing (and very little being), everyone is becoming disconnected from the most vital experience … which is to know oneself? Why has unscheduled, unstructured time for our kids become obsolete? How is it that we don't see how important being is to our doing? And what if we need to learn to be, not just do, to become who we are?

Take a moment to stop reading these words. Close your eyes and take a few slow deep breaths. Feel yourself disconnect from the world around you as you go within yourself. Feel the stillness between your thoughts. Feel the space. Therein lies the key to living with more presence, more consciousness, more clarity, and more being. None of which can be accessed from a non-stop treadmill of busyness. When we are occupied all the time, we become unplugged from our deeper, higher knowing, our awareness, and our guidance.

Our culture even has an acronym now—FOMO (fear of missing out)—to express our incredible preoccupation with busyness.

So, what is going on? Is this non-stop, busy lifestyle truly best for us? What are the consequences of living on a non-stop treadmill—for ourselves and our kids? These are important questions to be aware of, so that we are able to make decisions and choices with clarity and awareness for ourselves, our families, and even our communities.

To know oneself, we must be able to be quiet and be with ourselves. Therefore, in a life that never slows down, never has quiet space, it becomes impossible to connect to ourselves from within. We slowly lose connection with ourselves (or do not develop that muscle at all) if we never have space to be quiet during our childhoods. We actually become much more of a "human doing," than a human being. To do is a necessary part of life, but it is also necessary to *be*.

Take a few deep breaths. Disconnect from the world around you and see if you can feel yourself within your breath. Feel the stillness behind your thoughts. Notice the you within you. Therein lies the key to living with more presence, connection, consciousness, clarity, awareness, and power—none of which can be accessed from a non-stop treadmill of busyness. When we are occupied all the time, we become unplugged from our deeper, higher knowing and guidance. It is incredibly difficult (in a non-stop lifestyle) to hear oneself apart from the outside world. Additionally, our choices and responses to life then come from outside of us, rather than the truth within us.

We each need a balance of both doing and being. This is a balance that is never perfect, but instead, meant to shift and flow with our internal rhythms—which are different for each individual. The key is to connect with and know your own internal rhythm, which takes some time and attentiveness.

So, take some time to sit with these ideas, especially if they are new to you. Be gentle with your thoughts and feelings on this topic. Our society has strong beliefs surrounding productivity, many biases about slowing down, and FOMO … if we do choose to slow down. The question then becomes this: what if what we are really missing out on is never actually the doing … but instead, the experience of being?

Only you know the answers for yourself. Trust yourself and your ability to bring awareness to the concepts of both doing and being.

Why Am I Here?

Have you ever wondered why we're here on Earth? Or why we are here at this time, in this place? Have you ever wondered what life is for? Have you contemplated your own existence?

The question of our human existence has been contemplated since the beginning of thought. There are countless beliefs and perspectives about why we are here. However, for each of us, this question must be answered individually, if we are to connect and tap into meaning in our lives. Meaning is developed by us, not for us. Meaning is internal, not external. Meaning is beyond thought—what arises inside of the stillness. If you listen, it comes. The noise of life is not where meaning is found. Therein lies the root of much suffering.

The question "why am I here?" is the key that unlocks purpose, passions, intentions, and our conscious actions. Without this question, we can easily become lost in our own lives.

The question itself serves as an anchor; purpose and meaning create direction, tap us into our internal GPS, make our intentions clearer, and give our choices direction. Humans ponder the randomness of life. Once this question "why am I here?" is asked, it becomes more evident that what appeared to be randomness was simply a lack of awareness. It becomes clear that life is not random, it is perceived based on our current state of awareness. Without awareness, our lives are created by unconscious reactions rather than conscious creation. Everything comes from us, and then flows through us and is released out into the world.

This one question, "why am I here?", opens a door unlike any other. The answer to the question is far less important than just simply asking it. Just sit with the question. The question itself is the experience. Once you ask, listen carefully from within. Go beyond your mind-based thoughts and into your higher awareness. A quiet knowing begins to emerge. Be patient with yourself. This can take time.

Even with awareness, this question of why you are here will have layers of meaning to you at different stages of your life experience. The question is an opening. It is a bridge to a higher aspect of ourselves that knows there is more to life than just our day-to-day tasks. This is an invitation to go deeper within yourself, become comfortable with the question, and let answers unfold gently from within. They will. Be patient. Trust your inner knowing. Invite the clarity. Step out of the mind and out of your own way. This is the practice.

Without awareness,
our lives are created
by unconscious
reactions rather than
conscious creation.

Our Inherent Worth.

We are born with inherent worth. Each of us is a sacred being. We enter life completely dependent on those around us. Our parents or caregivers are our entire lifeline connecting (or disconnecting) us to that inherent worth through how our needs are met.

In the beginning, those needs are basic: nourishment, shelter, safety, sleep, and comfort. The message of our worth is received by those needs being met (or not). From there, as we individuate, our worth is felt, mirrored, and learned not just by having our basic needs met, but by how those around us treat and respond to us. We continually absorb behavior and energy that is directed toward us. This is not what creates our worthiness—because we are born with it—but it is what develops it, directs it, and sets the tone for our lives.

It is a sacred role to be the developer and director of the worthiness of a human life. And that is exactly what we are as parents and caregivers. The emotional generosity and love we choose to share—whether conditional or unconditional—sets the tone of worth in our children. This responsibility cannot be minimized. Our awareness as parents, and our reverence for our children's lives, can focus our intentions for how we navigate the roles we have been entrusted to undertake. And the worthiness our children feel is fostered through how we treat them.

Parenting concepts have been taught, discussed, debated, and pondered forever. Authoritarian concepts were the foundation of parenting for decades and decades, when our basic needs were primary and our consciousness was less aware.

Today, we are more aware. We have unlimited choices when deciding how we will influence, mold, and nurture life. People fiercely protect their beliefs about how to accomplish the task of parenting children. This will always be the case. But what if, instead of debating, comparing, judging, and condemning, we decide to intensely focus on this idea of worthiness.

Our worth is not determined by how people treat us—but it is deeply influenced, molded, and directed by it. Once you are aware you are a soul in a human body, you know your worth is inherent. You were born with tremendous worth, yet how you are treated can make that worth seem conditional. If you allow yourself to believe this, you will spend the rest of your life trying to *prove* your worth.

Your worth is inherent. Every human life has deep worth. Isn't it time we began to acknowledge and behave like this is true? And isn't it time we treated one another—and most especially our children—with reverence for this inherent worth? How about we begin to see with clear eyes how important it is that we value ourselves. As within, so without. We cannot give what we do not own. We must claim our inherent worth if we are to claim our power. They are one in the same.

The first step is to acknowledge and accept our individual, sacred worth; to heal the unworthiness we feel within ourselves. If we are not connected to our own inherent worth, we cannot see it in other people or nurture it in our children. Instead, we unintentionally pass onto others our own disconnection and feelings of unworthiness.

We heal the world by healing ourselves and then paying it forward.

Relation to Self, Relation to Others.

Relation is defined as an existing connection.

Relationship is the way in which two or more people are connected.

How is it that we make relationship (how we connect to others) more important than how we relate with ourselves? And is this really the most beneficial choice? Is it even a conscious choice?

Let's bring some greater awareness to this topic.

If we accept that we are souls in a human body—having an experience of ourselves—it would seem to follow that the way in which we relate to ourselves would be our greatest priority. Yet relationship to others takes the front seat. Additionally, we are more concerned about how others feel about us than how we feel about ourselves. Puzzling, isn't it?

Yes, we are creatures of connection. We want and need to connect to one another. We also need a connection to ourselves. But maybe, as we enter into the world completely dependent on others for our survival, relationship becomes primary to us—because at that point, it is. Once we begin to individuate—to see and know we are separate from others—we glimpse the possibility of connection to ourselves. We've all seen a toddler deeply engrossed in a world of their own, building blocks (as an example) with no need for anyone else. He is connected, not just to the activity, but also to himself. The same is true for us. We need the time and space to connect with ourselves. It is time that we need to carve out and prioritize if we want to be in our power.

As parents and caregivers, if we are to nurture this connection our children have to themselves, we not only need to model it with our own behavior and choices, but allow our children the quiet space and time to connect with themselves. However, this is most often not the case—especially now—in a world of non-stop activity and over-scheduled kids. This never-ending busyness blocks the connection our children have with themselves. But the time and space to tap into themselves is essential if their connection to themselves is going to be made, nurtured, and grow within them.

The way we relate to ourselves is the foundation of our relationships to others. How we love ourselves is the launching pad for how we love others. And how we care for our wellness and well-being is what we have (or do not have) have available for others. How we relate to ourselves is the foundation of how we relate with all others.

Still ... we are given the message that it is not. In fact, somehow, somewhere along the way, caring for oneself began to be seen as selfishness—tragic belief this is, for us all.

Take some time to observe (without judgment) how you relate with yourself. Encourage more connection with yourself. Take some time to yourself. Love yourself the way you love in the most important relationship in your life. Forgive yourself the way you forgive others. Be gentle with yourself the way you would an infant. After all, relating to yourself is what the soul longs for....

The Slippery Slope of Opinions.

In light of our awareness, clarity, and power, it is important to discuss the concept of opinions. We've all heard the expression "opinions are like a**holes—everybody's got one." Well, it is true that everybody's got one.

How important do you make opinions in your life? Do you collect opinions to feel better about the choices you make? Do you collect opinions to make your decisions? Do you choose to surround yourself with only people whose opinions match yours? What do you do when your opinions clash with others? Do you judge people's opinions? How do you treat people who have differing opinions? These are all good questions for increasing self-awareness.

The slippery slope of opinions lies in their external focus, rather than the internal focus of connection to ourselves. Opinions do not serve the connection to ourselves or our clarity. We can become lost and disconnected from ourselves if we choose to gather opinions. Further, if we choose to mold ourselves to fit the opinions of others, dim our voices, or shrink because of those opinions, we lose touch with our inner truths, guidance, clarity, and awareness. This is a huge price to pay for placing a focus on others' opinions. In truth, anyone else's opinion is irrelevant to you and may not serve your highest good.

Shedding more light on the concept of opinions in your world has the potential to increase your awareness and clarity about how you choose to live and be in the world. Do not give your power away by collecting opinions. The most important opinion of yourself, of what you do, who you are, and what you choose for yourself is your own.

Opinions do not
serve the
connection to
ourselves or
our clarity.

Recognizing Your Highest Good.

What is in your highest good? Do you know?

We are all capable of answering this question. However, whether it is easy or difficult to answer this question lies in our awareness of self, beyond the noise of the mind. We are each capable of opening our awareness to our highest good. It requires quieting our thoughts, focusing from within, and placing our interest, intention, and focus on the concept of highest good. It is amazing what comes when we ask and allow. Ask yourself to feel and sense more of your highest good in your daily choices. Place some focus on the idea of your highest good and observe what surfaces. Our inner knowing is a gentle nudge. It is a sense of what feels better.

Often we discover aspects of our highest good from the experiences we have that are very obviously not in our highest good! The human experience is one of contrast. We discover what is from what is not. Without these contrasting experiences, it is difficult to have clarity about our highest good. But once we do, and we bring awareness to those experiences, we develop clarity and the power to discern and choose those actions that align with our highest good. Those actions begin to feel inspired. They feel right. They fit for you and they fit that moment in time. This is what alignment is. It is the ability to take inspired actions that align with your highest good.

We certainly are not taught or guided by how we are raised to understand, feel, know, or connect to our highest good. Yet what could possibly be more vital to living a life that is authentic, fulfilling, and on our path if we do not know, understand, or connect to our highest good with each moment and choice? Our lives are based on the choices we make. If the choices we make are not made in our highest good, how can we expect to live in alignment, purpose, or have true happiness or fulfillment? Wherever you go, there you are.

This journey of life (a soul in a human body) is meant to be a connection to self first, and then those around us ... not the other way around. We are also capable (if we live in practice of highest good) of creating families that honor, consider, and choose to live and make decisions that serve everyone's highest good in the family. As parents, if we connect to, live, and honor our individual highest good, we can better connect, honor, understand, and choose the highest good for and with our children. A family harmony emerges through the honoring of each individual's highest good.

Remember: highest good resides beyond the mind. Your highest good is not something that can be figured out, measured, quantified, contemplated, debated, or researched. It is not something you can find by gathering opinions. Your highest good emerges from an inner connection to your highest self, to all that is, to the truth of who you are. It emerges easily once you become quiet. It is a muscle that needs developing and, once developed, becomes strong.

Allow yourself space for awareness to emerge. Remember the effort lies in creating an environment for the knowing to surface. The answers are already within you, and so too is your highest good. Trust yourself. You know who you are.

A Time of Awakening.

We are in a time of great awakening.

Our collective consciousness is rising.

The snow globe of untruths has been shaken in order for the truths to settle.

This is a time of major shifting and change.

We are all (whether we know it or not) awakening to higher consciousness—to our divinity, to the harmony that is achievable, to the oneness we all wish to live, and the unequivocal truths of our being.

Can you feel it?

Recognition of these shifts and changes not only in the world around you, but within you, is the beginning of your higher awareness.

You can't do awakening wrong, and you will never get it done—so your only job is to be willing.

The current chaos of the world is a representation of the healing that needs to occur in each of us.

And within each of us lies the power to heal, to be in harmony, to know our divinity, and to live our truth.

We are each here to wake up to the truth of who we are, and begin the process of healing our own inner wounds. Every bit of healing you do assists not only yourself, but the entire human collective.

We are all connected. Therefore, any and all healing, awareness, clarity, and power you create within yourself, your family, your circle, your community, emanates energetically out to us all. Yes. You are that powerful.

Yes, we are all that powerful.

And yes, that is how you help heal the world.

It is my greatest hope that you have come into a stronger sense of internal awareness, clarity, and power

End Notes.

Everything you need is inside of you. The key is becoming aware of your intrinsic knowing and acting on it consistently. You were born with the greatest GPS there is: internal guidance. It will not steer you wrong.

You've got this!
Jill

Want to dive deeper?

I would love to hear your thoughts about the book. Please contact me at info@awarenessclaritypower.com or visit my website awarenessclaritypower.com.